Cool Kid Businesses

Laura Hamilton Waxman

Lerner Publications ◆ Minneapolis

Lerner Publications Company
An imprint of Lerner Publishing Group, Inc.
241 First Avenue North
Minneapolis, MN 55401 USA

For reading levels and more information, look up this title at www.lernerbooks.com.

Library of Congress Cataloging-in-Publication Data

The Cataloging-in-Publication Data for *Cool Kid Businesses* is on file at the Library of Congress.
ISBN 978-1-5415-7700-8 (lib. bdg.)
ISBN 978-1-5415-8911-7 (pbk.)
ISBN 978-1-5415-8320-7 (eb pdf)

Manufactured in the United States of America
1-46722-47713-7/31/2019

Table of Contents

Bright Ideas

A good business starts with a great idea. But it takes more than an idea to run a business. It takes a lot of hard work.

Kid business owners are up for the challenge. They know how to make things that people will buy. And they know how to keep their companies going.

Food, Drink, and Treats

Do you like to bake or cook? Some kids have turned that skill into a successful business.

Cory has sold his cookies in stores and online.

Cory Nieves

Cory Nieves wanted to bake and sell cookies. He spent months getting his recipe just right. His idea turned into a company called Mr. Cory's Cookies. He is saving the money from his business for college.

Mikaila's company has made millions of dollars selling lemonade.

Mikaila Ulmer

Mikaila Ulmer used to be afraid of bees. Then she started Me & the Bees Lemonade. Her company makes lemonade with honey. She gives away some of her profits to keep Earth's honeybees safe.

Alina Morse

Alina Morse loves candy. But she knows it is bad for her teeth. At the age of nine, she figured out how to make lollipops without sugar. She called them Zollipops and started a company to sell them.

Alina donates 10% of her profits to teaching kids how to keep their teeth healthy and strong.

Fun Fashion

Do you like to wear cool clothes? These kids are designing and selling their own fashion lines.

Isabella Rose Taylor

Isabella Rose Taylor learned to sew one summer at camp. Then she started designing and selling her own clothes. Isabella has sold dresses, T-shirts, hoodies, and more.

Isabella makes clothes for preteens and teens.

Mo Bridges

Moziah (Mo) Bridges started his company when he was twelve. Mo's Bows makes cool and colorful bowties for kids and grown-ups. Mo's business even made bowties for the National Basketball Association.

Madison took regular flip-flops like these to a whole new level with her FishFlops.

Madison Robinson

Madison Robinson loves going to the beach. One day, she asked her dad to help her design beach sandals shaped like sea creatures. Madison called them FishFlops, and she has sold millions of them.

Science and Tech

Do you like to do science experiments? Or maybe you love to build things or learn about technology. Some kids turn their love of technology, science, and engineering into big business.

Thomas's new plan is to make and sell 3D printers.

Thomas Suarez

Thomas Suarez is a tech wizard. He started making software when he was just nine years old. Two years later, he started CarrotCorp. It makes and sells apps for phones.

Isabella Dymalovski

Isabella Dymalovski got her start when she was thirteen. She wanted to make skin care products that were safe for kids. She started experimenting with ingredients from nature.

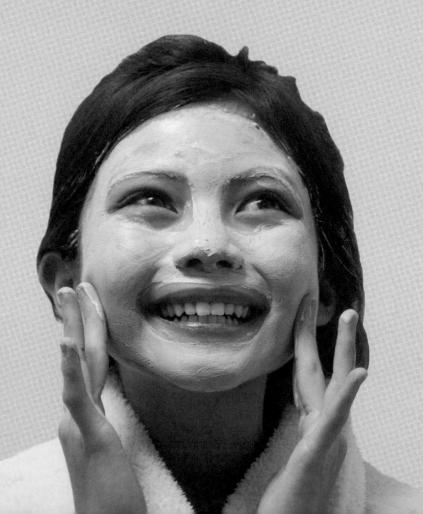

Isabella is from Australia and has sold her products all over the world.

Isabella founded Luv Ur Skin. Her company sells lotion, lip gloss, nail polish, and more. All her products are for kids and preteens.

Shubham Banerjee

Shubham Banerjee wanted to help blind people. So he started Braigo Labs. It makes printers that print Braille. Braille letters have raised dots that people can read with their fingers.

The kids in this book are business leaders. They're proving that young people can have big ideas. They are changing the world one product at a time.

You Can Do It!

Do you want to start a business? First, think about things you love to do or make. For example, you might like to walk dogs, make bracelets, or bake brownies. Next, think about how you could make money doing what you love. Start a dog-walking business. Or try selling bracelets or brownies in your neighborhood. You might start out with just a few customers. But keep at it. With hard work, you could have a real business.

Did You Know?

- Cory Nieves started out selling hot cocoa and lemonade. His mom had the idea to sell chocolate chip cookies instead.

- Madison Robinson has given away thousands of FishFlops to kids in hospitals and kids in military families.

- Isabella Rose Taylor was just thirteen when she took her clothes to New York Fashion Week. At this huge event, she and other designers put on fashion shows to present their work.

- Shubham Banerjee was in seventh grade when he came up with his idea for a Braille printer. It started out as a project for a science fair.

Glossary

design: to make a plan for how a new product will look

engineering: planning and making machines or objects

founded: started a new business

product: something that is made to sell to others

profit: the money that a business earns

software: programs made for computers

technology: scientific inventions and other tools that change how people live

Further Reading

FishFlops
https://fishflops.com

Luv Ur Skin
https://luvurskin.com

Me & the Bees Lemonade
https://www.meandthebees.com/pages/about-us

Mr. Cory's Cookies
https://mrcoryscookies.com/pages/our-story

Owen, Ruth. *I Can Start a Business!* New York: Windmill Books, 2018.

60 Small Business Ideas for Teenagers & Kids
https://moneypantry.com/kids-business-ideas/

Waxman, Laura Hamilton. *Cool Kid Inventions*. Minneapolis: Lerner Publications, 2020.

Index

Photo Acknowledgments

Image credits: iStock/Getty Images, pp. 2, 13; New Africa/Shutterstock.com, p. 4; WeAre/Shutterstock.com, p. 5; Studio Romantic/Shutterstock.com, p. 6; D Dipasupil/ Getty Images, p. 7; Jim Benett/Getty Images, p. 8; Michael Bezjian/Getty Images, p. 9; In Green/Shutterstock.com, p. 10; Sarah Edwards/Alamy Stock Photo, p. 11; Greg Doherty/ Getty Images, p. 12; Yuriy Golub/Shutterstock.com, p. 14; Noam Galai/Getty Images, p. 15; Terry Vine/Getty Images, p. 16; Iryna Tiumentseva/Shutterstock.com, p. 17; Patrick Tehan/ Alamy Stock Photo, p. 18; Ranta Images/Shutterstock.com, p. 19; Vinicius Tupinamba/ Shutterstock.com, p. 23.

Cover Image: D Dipasupil/Getty Images.

Main body text set in Billy Infant regular. Typeface provided by SparkType.